six folk tales

Adapted by Sheila Lane
and Marion Kemp
from the stories by Leila Berg

Take Part Series

Ward Lock Educational Co. Ltd.

six folk tales

Adapted by Sheila Lane
and Marion Kemp
from the stories by Leila Berg

Illustrations by Colin Smithson

1 Christopher Road
East Grinstead
Sussex RH19 3BT

A member of the Ling Kee Group
London • Hong Kong • New York • Singapore

First published by Brockhampton Press Limited 1966
This adaptation first published by Penguin Books 1973
This adaptation published by
Ward Lock Educational Co. Ltd. 1976

Reprinted 1987, 1991

ISBN 0 7062 3496 0

Printed in Hong Kong.

contents

★ *This sign means that you can make the sounds which go with the story.*

the soup-stone

This story is told by:
Old Man and
Good Woman

OLD MAN I am a very poor man. But I can get soup from a stone, so I don't go hungry. Now this is the way I do it: I bend myself down and pick up a stone from the roadway. Then I knock at a door, like this. ★

Good morning to you, Good Woman!

GOOD WOMAN Good morning to you.

OLD MAN Have you ever seen a stone like this before?

GOOD WOMAN No, what is it?

OLD MAN Oh, it's my soup-stone.

GOOD WOMAN What is a soup-stone?

OLD MAN It's a stone for making soup, of course.

GOOD WOMAN Oh no, no, no, no! A stone can't make soup.

OLD MAN Oh yes it can! A soup-stone like this can make really good soup. You may never have heard of such a thing, but I can tell you, a soup-stone like this can make really good soup.

GOOD WOMAN Oh no, no, no! A soup-stone can't make good soup.

OLD MAN Oh yes it can! It makes wonderful soup. I'll tell you what. If you will let me come in and lend me a pan, I'll show you how to do it.

GOOD WOMAN Come in. Come in and I'll lend you a pan. Here you are, but a soup-stone can't make good soup.

OLD MAN Well, you have to put the stone at the bottom of the pan like this, ★ and cover it with water like this. Help me to stir. ★ Hmm! Hmm! Lovely, lovely soup! Boil away, soup, boil away. Don't worry, Good Woman, it will soon be ready.

GOOD WOMAN Oh no, no! A soup-stone can't make good soup. Is it ready yet?

OLD MAN Oh no, not yet, but it's going to be gorgeous soup. It will be the most delicious soup you have ever tasted. Just one thing . . . have you got such a thing as a carrot?

GOOD WOMAN Yes, I have. I've got a carrot.

OLD MAN Well, if you put it in the soup, it will bring out the flavour.

GOOD WOMAN I will go and get the carrot. ★ Here it is.

OLD MAN Help me to stir. ★ Hmm! Hmm! Lovely, lovely soup. Boil away soup, boil away. Don't worry, Good Woman, it will soon be ready.

GOOD WOMAN Is it ready yet?

OLD MAN Oh no, but it's going to be gorgeous soup. It's going to be the most delicious soup you ever tasted. Just one thing . . . have you got such a thing as an onion?

GOOD WOMAN Yes, I have. I've got an onion.

OLD MAN Well, an onion would make it better still. It's gorgeous soup, but an onion would bring out the full flavour.

GOOD WOMAN I will go and get the onion. ★ Here it is.

OLD MAN Help me to stir. ★ Hmm! Hmm! Lovely, lovely soup. Boil away soup, boil away.
Don't worry, Good Woman, it will soon be ready.

GOOD WOMAN Is it ready yet?

OLD MAN Nearly! Take a good smell. ★ Doesn't it smell good?

GOOD WOMAN It smells good. ★ Yes, it smells good.

OLD MAN Put some pepper and salt in. Go on, shake in lots of pepper and salt.

GOOD WOMAN It smells good. ★ It must be ready now.

OLD MAN No! Just one more thing. It's gorgeous soup. It will be the most delicious soup you have ever tasted, if you put in one last thing . . . have you got such a thing as a chicken?

GOOD WOMAN Yes, I have. I've got a chicken.

OLD MAN Well, a chicken would make it better still. It's gorgeous, delicious soup, but a chicken would bring out the full flavour.

GOOD WOMAN I will go and get the chicken. ★ Here it is.

OLD MAN Let's stir together. ★ Hmm! Hmm! Lovely soup! You have a stir on your own. ★

GOOD WOMAN Hmm! Hmm! Lovely soup!

OLD MAN Now then, we'll take out the chicken bones, and leave the soup a little longer. The soup-stone has to boil just that little bit longer, because as I said, it's the stone that really brings out the proper flavour.

GOOD WOMAN It smells good. ★ I wish I had a soup-stone like that.

OLD MAN Let's taste it. You taste it first. I bet it tastes wonderful. ★

GOOD WOMAN Hmm! Hmm! It tastes wonderful. I do wish I had a soup-stone like that.

OLD MAN This soup-stone makes the most gorgeous, delicious soup in the world. Isn't it wonderful?

GOOD WOMAN It's wonderful. I wish I had a soup-stone like that. I wish I could have gorgeous, delicious soup like this all the time.

OLD MAN Well, I'll tell you what I will do. You have been very kind to me, so I'll give you mine, my very own soup-stone. Perhaps I shall be able to get another one for myself.

GOOD WOMAN Oh, Old Man, how good of you! Now I have a soup-stone of my own, so I can make gorgeous, delicious soup all the time.

OLD MAN Well, I'll be off. ★ Good-bye to you, good-bye.

GOOD WOMAN Good-bye. Good-bye. Thank you for the soup-stone.

OLD MAN And tomorrow, when I'm hungry, do you know what I'll do?
I'll bend myself down,
and pick up a _ _ _ _ _,
then I'll knock on a _ _ _ _,
and I'll say, _ _ _ _ _ _ _ _ _ _ _ _ _ _ _ _ _.

You might be lucky enough to get his next soup-stone!

Anansi and the Pudding Tree

This story is told by:
Anansi
Mouse and
Kisander

ANANSI I am Anansi, the spider.
And I have a friend called Mouse.

MOUSE That's me.

KISANDER And I am Kisander the cat. I am friends with myself.

ALL Now this is the tale of puddings that grow on trees. And this is the way we tell it.

ANANSI I would love one of those puddings that grow on your tree, Kisander.

MOUSE And so would I.

ANANSI But I am so frightened of your sharp teeth and your sharp claws, Kisander.

MOUSE And so am I.

ANANSI You can pounce very quickly.

MOUSE And you can see in the dark.

ANANSI Then we don't know you're there, Kisander.

KISANDER Psstt! Psstt! You have woken me up!★ Mee-ow!

ANANSI Oh dear! Don't start making your horrible waily-waily noise, Kisander, and don't wave your tail in the air like that.

MOUSE No, don't wave your tail in the air like that, Kisander.

ANANSI We would like one of your puddings, so please can we help you to clear the weeds away from your pudding tree?

MOUSE Kisander! Kisander! Can we help you to clear the weeds away from the pudding tree?

KISANDER Psstt! Psstt! My puddings are big and round and sweet. The bigger and rounder they grow, the more I want them for myself. Mee-ow! Mee-ow! ★

ANANSI Can we help you to water the pudding tree all round?

MOUSE Please let us help you, Kisander.

KISANDER Psstt! Psstt! You want to help yourselves to my big, round, sweet puddings. Mee-ow! Mee-ow! ★ I'm going to sleep, so leave my puddings alone.

ANANSI Come away, Mouse. ★ Now, let's wait until Kisander is asleep, then we'll TAKE some puddings.

MOUSE How can we take Kisander's puddings, Anansi?

ANANSI I'll climb up the tree and cut off the puddings with my sharp knife. You can stay at the bottom of the tree and tell me if Kisander is coming.

MOUSE How shall I tell you if Kisander is coming, Anansi?

ANANSI You mustn't call out, 'Anansi', because then Kisander will know who it is who is stealing her puddings.

MOUSE What shall I call out then, Anansi?

ANANSI You must call me, 'Ceiling Thomas'. You must call me 'Ceiling Thomas', because I am a spider and walk on the ceiling. Come on, Mouse, let's go back to Kisander's tree. ★ Creep softly, so that we don't wake her.

MOUSE You go up the tree, Anansi, and I will call out if Kisander comes.

ANANSI Don't forget that you must call me 'Ceiling Thomas'. I'll cut the pudding now. Are you ready?

MOUSE Yes, I'm ready . . . ★ Plop!

ANANSI Keep quiet, Mouse. That loud plop will wake Kisander up.

KISANDER Psstt! Psstt! What's happening in my garden? ★ What's happening to my puddings? The wind must be blowing them down. Never mind! I'll turn over and go to sleep again.

ANANSI It's all right, Mouse. I'll cut another pudding. But remember to call out, 'Ceiling Thomas', if Kisander comes. Ready?

MOUSE Yes, cut another pudding and if Kisander comes I'll call out 'Ceiling Thomas'.

ANANSI I'll cut the pudding now. Are you ready?

MOUSE Yes, I'm ready . . . ★ PLOP!

ANANSI Keep quiet, Mouse. Don't call out unless Kisander is coming.

KISANDER Psstt! Psstt! What's happening in my garden? ★ What's happening to my puddings? They are falling off the tree all by themselves. They must be too ripe. Oh never mind! I'm tired, I'll go to sleep again.

MOUSE Cut one more pudding, Anansi, just one more. ★ P-L-O-P!

KISANDER Psstt! Psstt! There is another plop. This time I shall go and see just what is happening to my puddings. ★

MOUSE Oh dear! I must call Anansi. Oh dear, I must call him . . .! Let me think . . . Oh yes! Ceiling Thomas! Ceiling Thomas!

ANANSI Sh! Sh! I'll curl up in a ball, as quiet as quiet in the leaves of the pudding tree. Sssh! Sssh! Be off on your trickly little feet, Mouse.

MOUSE Yes, I'll be off! ★

KISANDER Psstt! Psstt! Someone *has* been cutting my puddings, but I can't see anyone at all. One . . . two . . . three puddings. I'm not going to leave these puddings here. I'll take them back to the house.

ANANSI She's gone! Kisander has gone back into the house, so down I jump with a great big P-L-O-P! ★

KISANDER Psstt! Psstt! That was another pudding going plop! I'll go and see who is taking my puddings. ★ Well! What a strange thing! I can't see another pudding, but I heard a plop.
A PLOP! But no pudding!
A PLOP! BUT NO PUDDING!

And Kisander never found out what had made that last plop of all.

the Billy-Goats Gruff

This story is told by:
Big Billy-Goat Gruff
Second Billy-Goat Gruff
Little Billy-Goat Gruff and
The Troll

THE THREE GOATS This is the tale of The Three Billy-Goats Gruff.

LITTLE BILLY I'm Little Billy-Goat Gruff.

SECOND BILLY I'm Second Billy-Goat Gruff.

BIG BILLY I'm Big Billy-Goat Gruff.

THREE GOATS This is the tale of The Three Billy-Goats Gruff. And this is the way we tell it. . . .

TROLL Don't forget about me!

THREE GOATS Who are you?

TROLL I'm the Troll with eyes as big as saucers and a nose as big as a poker.

THREE GOATS Where do you live?

TROLL I live under the bridge, down by the little river.

LITTLE BILLY But we have to go over that bridge . . .

SECOND BILLY . . . to get to the hill . . .

BIG BILLY . . . where there is juicy, green grass to make us fat.

TROLL I don't care about that!
I live under the bridge, so keep away. I'm going home now. ★

SECOND BILLY We must look out for that Troll.

BIG BILLY Or he will gobble us up.

LITTLE BILLY But I must have some grass, so I'm off!★

SECOND BILLY Look out for that Troll, Little Billy. Look out!

TROLL Who's that running trip-trap, trip-trap on to my bridge? ★

LITTLE BILLY It's only me, the Little Billy-Goat Gruff. I'm going on to the hillside to eat the juicy, green grass to make myself fat.

TROLL I don't care about that!
Don't you dare come on to my bridge, or I'll gobble you up.

LITTLE BILLY Oh, don't gobble me up. I'm much too little.
Eat my brother, he's much bigger than me.
He's just coming now. ★

TROLL Oh, all right, I'll do that. I'll let you go over and I'll have your brother for dinner instead.

BIG BILLY Little Billy hasn't come back, so he must be eating the juicy, green grass.

SECOND BILLY Look! There's Little Billy. He's over on the hillside. I must have some juicy, green grass, so I'm going too! ★

TROLL Who's that running TRIP-TRAP TRIP-TRAP on to my bridge? ★

SECOND BILLY It's me, the Second Billy-Goat Gruff. I'm going on to the hillside to eat the juicy, green grass to make myself fat.

TROLL I don't care about that!
Don't you dare come on to my bridge, or I'll gobble you up.

SECOND BILLY Oh, don't gobble me up. I'm much too little.
Eat my brother, he's bigger than me.
He's just coming now. ★

TROLL Oh, all right, I'll do that. I'll let you go over and I'll have your big brother for dinner instead.

BIG BILLY I'm already big and fat, but I must have some juicy, green grass to make myself bigger and fatter. I can see Little Billy and Second Billy on the hillside, so I'm going too. I'm going over the bridge to the hillside to get some of that juicy, green grass for myself. ★

TROLL Who's that running TRIP-TRAP, TRIP-TRAP on to my bridge?★

BIG BILLY It's ME. I'm the biggest and fattest Billy-Goat Gruff. I'm big and I'm fat and I'm going over your bridge and up to the hillside, to get some of the juicy, green grass to make myself bigger and fatter.

TROLL Big and fat!
We'll see about that.
Bigger and fatter!
That doesn't matter.
Don't you dare come on to my bridge, or I'll gobble you up!

BIG BILLY Gobble me up! Gobble me up! Oh no you won't. I'll run at you with my long horns and I'll toss you up in the air. ★

SECOND BILLY Toss him up in the air, Big Billy.

BIG BILLY I'll toss him up in the air and I'll toss him down in the water. ★

LITTLE BILLY Toss him up into the air, then down into the water, so that he's never seen again. ★

SECOND BILLY Come on over the bridge, Big Billy, and help us to eat the juicy, green grass. ★

BIG BILLY That's it! We'll all eat the juicy green grass and get fatter . . .

SECOND BILLY AND FATTER......

LITTLE BILLY AND FATTER!

And the three Billy-Goats Gruff got so fat they could scarcely get home again.

the woman who always argued

This story is told by:
The Old Man
The Old Woman and
The Old Man's Friend

OLD MAN I'm the Old Man and I'm all right.

FRIEND I'm the Old Man's Friend and I'm all right.

OLD MAN But I've got an Old Woman and she's NOT all right. She's a trouble. This is the tale of my Old Woman who always argues. That's how she makes the trouble.

BOTH And this is the way we tell it.

OLD MAN When the fishmonger says that he's got some good herrings . . .

FRIEND Your Old Woman says . . .

BOTH No, I want some sprats.

OLD MAN When the butcher says that he's got some lamb chops . . .

FRIEND Your Old Woman says . . .

BOTH No, I want some beef.

OLD MAN When someone opens the window . . .

FRIEND Your Old Woman says . . .

BOTH Shut it!

OLD MAN When someone shuts the window . . .

FRIEND Your Old Woman says . . .

BOTH Open it!

OLD MAN When she looks at our hens . . .

FRIEND Your Old Woman says . . .

BOTH Look at our ducks!

OLD MAN When she looks at our cats . . .

FRIEND Your Old Woman Says. . . .

BOTH Look at our dogs!

OLD MAN When it rains . . .

FRIEND Your Old Woman says . . .

BOTH Look at the snow!

OLD MAN Whatever anyone says, she always says the opposite.

FRIEND And here she comes! ★

OLD WOMAN I'm going over the bridge to look at our cornfield. ★ Come on, Old Man.

OLD MAN Ah! The corn will be ready to cut by Tuesday.

OLD WOMAN No, it won't! The corn will be ready to cut by Monday.

FRIEND I knew she'd say that.

OLD MAN Very well then, Monday, I'll get John and Eric to help harvest it.

OLD WOMAN No you won't. You'll get James and Robert.

FRIEND I knew she'd say that.

OLD MAN All right. I'll get James and Robert. We'll start at seven o'clock.

OLD WOMAN No we won't. We'll start at six.

FRIEND I knew she'd say that.

OLD MAN All right. We'll start at six o'clock. The weather will be good then.

OLD WOMAN No it won't. It will be bad. It will rain.

FRIEND I knew she'd say that.

OLD MAN Well, whether it rains or shines, whether I get John or James, whether we do it on Monday at seven or Tuesday at six, we'll cut it with scythes.

OLD WOMAN No we won't. We'll cut it with shears.

FRIEND I knew she'd say that.

OLD MAN What are you talking about, you silly Old Woman? If you cut corn with shears, you have to bend down and go snip, snip at one tiny bit after another. But if you cut with a lovely, curved scythe, you go S-W-O-O-S-H and half the corn falls down flat. We'll cut it with scythes.

OLD WOMAN Shears!

OLD MAN Scythes!

FRIEND Look out, Old Woman! Look where you are going.

OLD MAN Look out, you silly Old Woman, or you'll fall over the bridge and into the water.

OLD WOMAN Shears!

OLD MAN She's going, she's going, she's GONE! ★ She's disappeared under the water.

FRIEND She's coming up again. ★

OLD WOMAN SHEARS!

OLD MAN SCYTHES! You stupid Old Woman. Look at her fingers going snip, snip above the water.

FRIEND She's going down again. ★

OLD MAN You stupid, obstinate Old Woman.

FRIEND She's coming up again. ★

OLD MAN There's so much water in her mouth, she can't keep opening it to argue, so her fingers are just going snip, snip above the water.

FRIEND She's going down again. ★

OLD MAN Now she's gone for good, the stupid, obstinate Old Woman. I suppose we'd better search in the water and see if we can find her. ★

FRIEND She isn't here.

OLD MAN If the water has carried her away, she will be downstream. Come on, ★ this is the way the river flows, and everything in the water must go with the river.

FRIEND She isn't here.

OLD MAN What a fool I am! Everything else in the water would go with the river it's true. But not my Old Woman! She's bound to do the opposite. She'll be floating the other way, mark my words!

FRIEND Let's run the other way. Let's run up, not down. ★

OLD MAN That's it, she's sure to float the opposite way to everything else.

FRIEND There she is! There she is!

OLD MAN Well, what do you know! My stupid, obstinate Old Woman is floating right UP the waterfall.

But don't you try it!

Rabbit and Elephant

This story is told by:
Rabbit
Elephant and
Farmer

RABBIT I'm Rabbit, and I have a friend called Elephant.

ELEPHANT I'm Elephant, and I have a friend called Rabbit.

FARMER I'm Farmer, and I have a pot of fine beans.

ALL This is the tale of a pot of fine beans,
And this is the way we tell it.

RABBIT Farmer, Farmer, will you give us some of your beans to eat if we work in your fields?

FARMER Yes, if you work in my fields, you can have this pot of fine beans.

ELEPHANT We'll work in your fields, Farmer. We'll work really hard. You know me, I'm Elephant!

FARMER Oh yes, I know you, Elephant!

RABBIT We'll work in the fields, while the beans are cooking away in the pot. Come on, Elephant, we must work hard in Farmer's field, ★ then he'll give us some of his beans.

ELEPHANT It's a bit hard on me to have to work like this. My foot hurts and my ear hurts and the grass prickles and something is biting me.

RABBIT Come on Elephant. Farmer has given us the beans, so we must do the work.

ELEPHANT Well, I suppose we must. I know! I'll just go and get myself a little drink and then I'll be back. ★

RABBIT Oh dear! It's very hard work, but I'll soon be finished.

FARMER How are you getting on with all the work, Rabbit? Your beans are cooking away in the pot.

RABBIT There's not much left to do now, Farmer.

ELEPHANT Here I am, Rabbit. ★ Now I do feel better. Oh look, you've nearly finished, and look how much I have left to do!

RABBIT Oh dear, I suppose I'll have to help you, or you'll never get finished.

ELEPHANT Help me out this time, Rabbit, while I go and get some banana leaves to cool my poor forehead and then I'll be back. ★

RABBIT Those beans do smell good. ★ I'm so hungry and hot and I've finished all the work, so I'll call Farmer. Farmer! Farmer! Are our beans ready yet?

FARMER Your beans are cooking away in the pot, Rabbit, just like I said.

ELEPHANT Here I am, Rabbit. ★ Now I feel better. Oh look, there's nothing left to do in the fields. But don't take any beans yet, I must just go and have a wash. You won't start without me, will you, because that isn't polite?

RABBIT No, of course I won't start without you, Elephant. I'll just have a little sleep until you come back. ★

ELEPHANT Ha-ha! Now I'll show him. I'll undo the buttons of my coat and step right out of it. One leg . . . two legs . . . three legs . . . four legs. RRRRRaaah! Now look at me. Did you know that Elephants are stripy monsters under their coats? RRRRRRaaah! I'll go back to the beans and frighten Rabbit away.

RRRRRaaah! ★

RABBIT Aaah! There's a monster rushing at me! It's as big as an elephant, but it doesn't look like an elephant at all.

FARMER A monster as big as an elephant! Listen to his roaring! ★ Run little Rabbit, run. ★

ELEPHANT RRRRRaaah! ★

RABBIT I'll hide in the grass till the monster has gone

FARMER It's all right, Rabbit. The monster has gone. But so have the beans!

RABBIT Oh dear! And now Elephant is coming back from the river. ★ He looks very happy too.

ELEPHANT Are the beans ready?

RABBIT Oh Elephant, a terrible thing happened. A monster has come and eaten all the beans.

FARMER Yes, a monster came and Rabbit ran and hid in the grass.

ELEPHANT I don't believe it. You've eaten them yourself, Rabbit.

RABBIT Oh no, you know I wouldn't.

ELEPHANT Well it can't be helped.

RABBIT But I'm hungry. I want some beans.

FARMER If you do some more work in my fields, I'll give you some more beans.

RABBIT Fetch another pot of beans, Farmer, and we'll do some more work in the fields while they are cooking.

ELEPHANT It's a bit hard on me, to have to work like this. ★ My toe is all blistered, my tail is all bent and I've got something in my eye. I know! I'll just go and get myself a little drink and then I'll be back. ★

RABBIT Oh dear, I suppose I'll have to do the work again. ★ I'm so hungry and hot, but I've nearly finished the work, so I'll call Farmer. Farmer! Farmer! Are our beans ready yet?

FARMER Your beans are cooking away in the pot, Rabbit, just like before.

RABBIT Well, I can't start without Elephant, so I'll just have a little sleep until he comes back. ★

ELEPHANT RRRRRaaah! ★

RABBIT Aaah! That monster's rushing at me again.

FARMER Oh, it's the monster that looks as big as an Elephant! Listen to his roaring! ★ Run little Rabbit, run. ★

ELEPHANT RRRRRaaah! ★

RABBIT I'll hide in the grass till the monster has gone.

FARMER It's all right, Rabbit. The monster has gone. But so have the beans!

RABBIT Oh dear! And now Elephant is coming back from the river. ★ He looks very happy too.

ELEPHANT Are the beans ready?

RABBIT Oh Elephant, a terrible thing has happened again. The monster came back and ate all the beans.

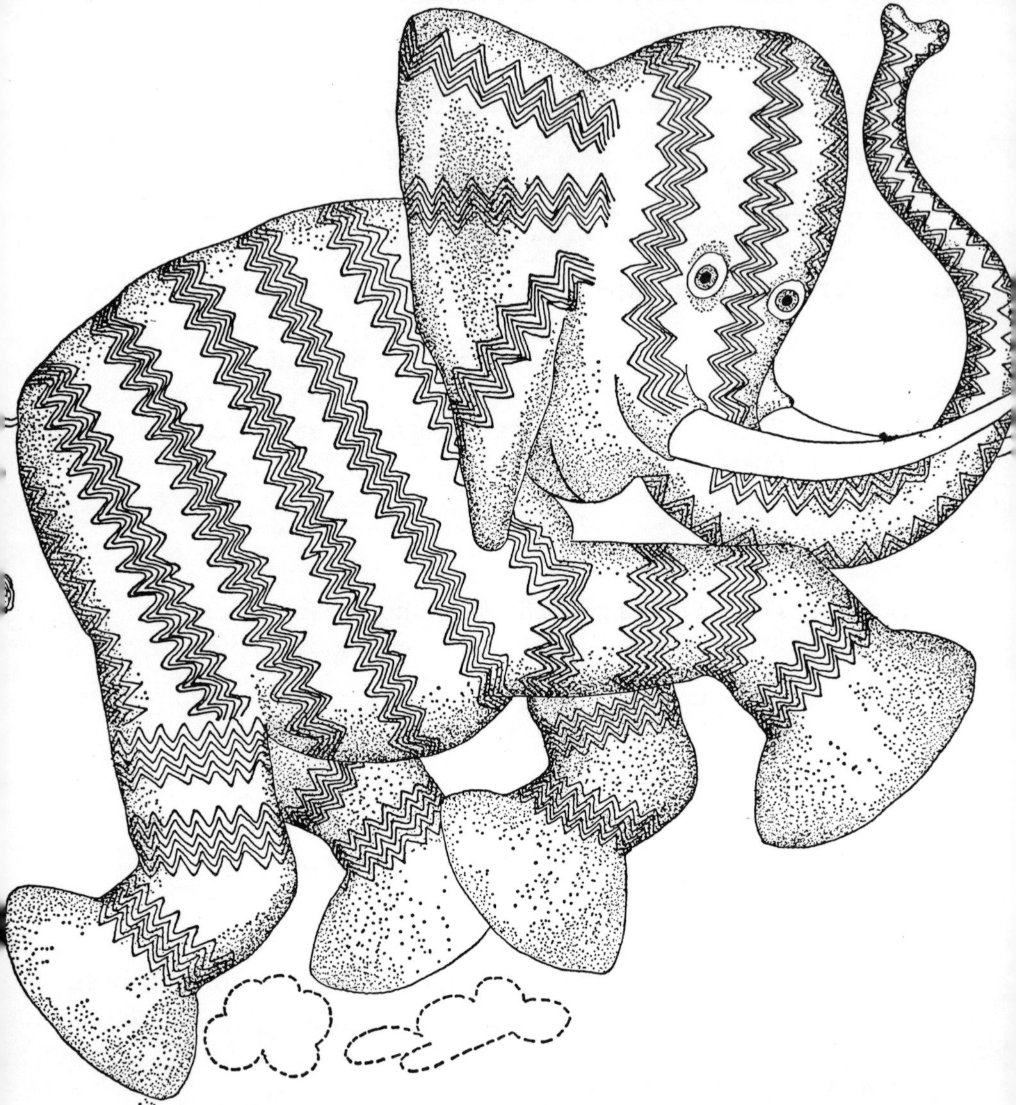

FARMER Yes, the monster came back, and Rabbit ran and hid in the grass.

ELEPHANT I bet you ate them yourself, Rabbit.

RABBIT No, I didn't. You know I didn't. I would never do a thing like that.

ELEPHANT Well, it can't be helped.

RABBIT It can be helped. Do you know what I'm going to do? I'm going to get my bow and arrow and if he comes again to take our beans, I'll shoot him dead.

FARMER That's it, Rabbit. You shoot him dead if he comes back again.

ELEPHANT I know a lot about bows and arrows, Rabbit. Let me look at your bow and I can tell you if it's a good one.

FARMER Let Elephant have a look at your bow, Rabbit.

ELEPHANT Mmmmn. Not bad at all. There's just a little bit here I'll make right for you. I'll cut it here. ★ Ah, that's better. That will be all right now. I'm glad you showed me your bow.

RABBIT Farmer, Farmer, can we have some more beans if we do some more work?

FARMER If you do some more work in my fields, I'll give you some more beans.

ELEPHANT It's a bit hard on me to have to work like this. ★ My head is so hot again. I know! I'll just go and get a little drink and then I'll be back. ★

RABBIT Oh dear! I have to do all the work again, and I am so hungry and hot. I've nearly finished the work, so I'll call Farmer. Farmer! Farmer! Are our beans ready yet?

ELEPHANT RRRRRaaah! ★

RABBIT Now I'll get you! I'll shoot you dead with my bow and arrow. Ow! My bow's broken. ★

FARMER Run little Rabbit, run. That monster's not dead but your bow is broken.

RABBIT Yes, and it's broken just in the place where Elephant cut it with his knife. We'll wait till that Elephant comes back from the river.

FARMER Here comes Elephant, back from the river. ★

ELEPHANT Did you catch the monster, Rabbit?

RABBIT No, the bow broke.

ELEPHANT Really, I am surprised.

RABBIT Are you? Are you really surprised, Elephant? Well, I'm going to have one more try to catch that monster.

FARMER And I'll give you some more beans if you do just a little more work.

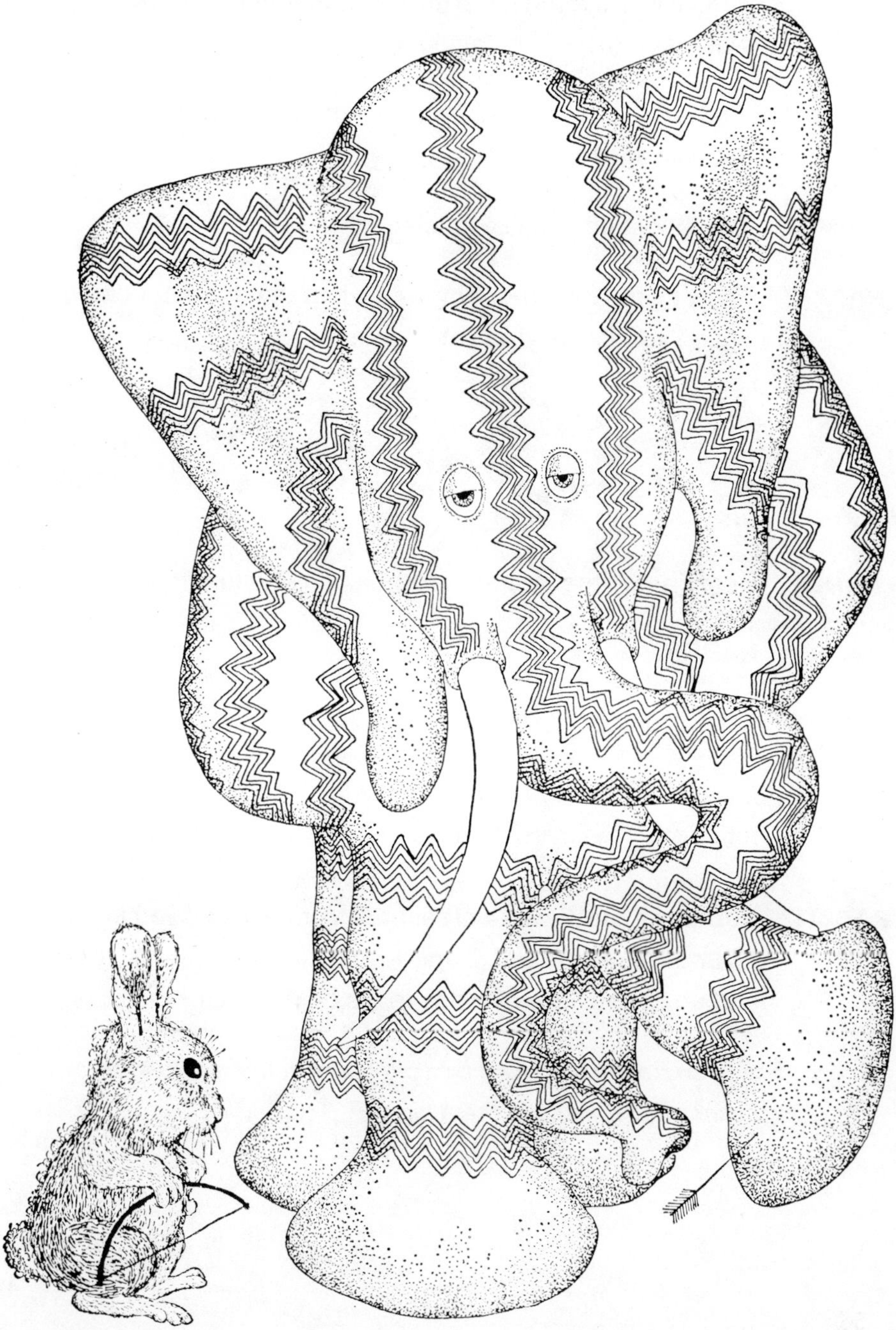

ELEPHANT You can do what you like. When I think about work, I feel tired and sick and thirsty. I'm going off to the river to have another wash and then I'll be back. ★

RABBIT Farmer, tell me something. Did you think that monster looked just like an elephant?

FARMER Yes, it looked just like an elephant.

RABBIT Then I'll get my other bow and when that monster comes back again, you'll see what you'll see!

FARMER Here comes the monster, Rabbit. It's coming now. ★

ELEPHANT RRRRRaaah! ★

RABBIT One . . . TWO. . . THREE . . . PING! ★

ELEPHANT Owww! You horrid thing, you've hurt me. What did you do that for? Fancy being so mean just for a few beans. I'll probably die.

RABBIT You won't die. It was only a prick. A fine friend you are. Now go and wash yourself properly this time, and put on your coat, and don't you dare play any tricks on me again!

And so Rabbit sat down by a big pot of bubbling, steaming beans and, at last, ate them all up.

Uncle Bouki and the Horse

This story is told by:
Uncle Bouki
Mean Old Man and
Clever Dick

ALL Now this is the tale of a trick that was played. But who was it played on?

UNCLE BOUKI I'm Uncle Bouki. Was it played on me?

MEAN OLD MAN I'm Mean Old Man. Was it played on me?

CLEVER DICK I'm Clever Dick. Was it played on me?

ALL This is the tale of a trick that was played.
We'll find out who it was played on.

UNCLE BOUKI What shall I do? I've got to get my fruit to market, but my donkey has run away. How can I get my yams to market now that I haven't got a donkey?

MEAN OLD MAN If the donkey has run away, you will have to carry all those yams yourself.

UNCLE BOUKI But I can't carry them all myself. Oh dear! I just don't know what to do.

MEAN OLD MAN Well, I've got a horse I can lend you, but I won't lend him for nothing. If I lend you my horse, you will have to give me fifty pence.

UNCLE BOUKI But I haven't got fifty pence.

MEAN OLD MAN Well, give me twenty pence now, and you can give me the other thirty pence when you come to collect the horse. And *see that you don't load him up too much!*

UNCLE BOUKI Here you are. Here's the twenty pence now and I'll bring the other thirty when I come to collect him. ★ Oh dear, oh dear, I knew this would cost me something, but I must get my yams to market.

CLEVER DICK Hi there, Uncle Bouki! What are you grumbling about?

UNCLE BOUKI I've lost my donkey and I've got to pay the Mean Old Man fifty pence for his horse, so that I can take my yams to market.

SWAG

CLEVER DICK But your donkey is back in the field. I've just seen her rolling about in the coffee plants to stop her back from tickling.

UNCLE BOUKI Oh dear, oh dear, and I've just paid the Mean Old Man twenty pence.

CLEVER DICK You've paid twenty pence to borrow a horse you don't need! You are in a jam, Uncle Bouki. That Mean Old Man will never give it back.

UNCLE BOUKI You're right. He'll never give it back. He's much too mean.

CLEVER DICK Listen, Uncle Bouki. I'll get your money back. You can rely on me. We'll go and see Mean Old Man together. Come on. ★

UNCLE BOUKI That's good of you, Clever Dick, but I don't know how you will do it.

CLEVER DICK Leave it to me. Let's knock on the door. ★ Good morning, Mean Old Man. We've come for the horse.

MEAN OLD MAN Give me the other thirty pence first.

CLEVER DICK Wait a bit. Bring him over here, so that we can have a look and see if he is big enough. ★

MEAN OLD MAN He's big enough. A horse is a horse, not an elephant. And remember, *see you don't load him up too much*.

CLEVER DICK Just a minute. We must measure him first. Now, there's twenty centimetres for Uncle Bouki, in the middle. There's sixteen centimetres for me. There's another twenty centimetres for my mammy at the front. And there's twenty-two centimetres for Auntie Bouki at the back, for she's fatter even than my mammy.

MEAN OLD MAN What are you talking about? You can't put four people on one horse!

CLEVER DICK Sssh! Don't muddle me. And here, on the horse's neck, there's twelve centimetres for young John. And – that's lucky – we can just fit the children in John's arms without taking up one more centimetre.

MEAN OLD MAN You're crazy!

UNCLE BOUKI What about the other children, Clever Dick?

CLEVER DICK Oh! They can sit between the horse's ears. One . . . two . . . three. . . . Yes, they can just squeeze in if they don't mind sitting pretty tight.

MEAN OLD MAN No, no! I don't want my horse loaded up too much.

UNCLE BOUKI What about the baby, Clever Dick? I can't see where to put the baby.

CLEVER DICK I think . . . yes . . . we'll have to roll him up in a blanket and tie him on to the horse's tail.

MEAN OLD MAN You can't tie a baby on my horse's tail!

CLEVER DICK Sssh! Don't muddle me. That's the second time I've had to tell you. I still haven't worked out where to put the pigs and goats. Ah yes! I can see what to do. We'll put the pigs in one sack and the goats in another sack, and we'll hang them one on each side of the horse.

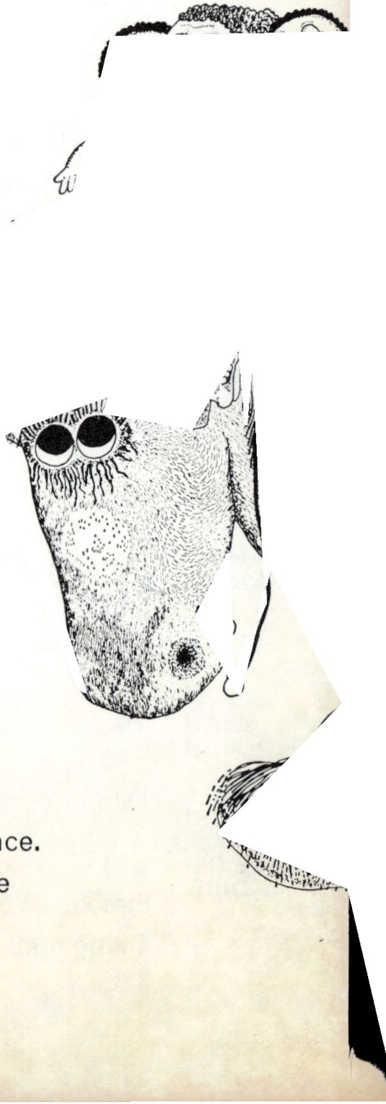

MEAN OLD MAN That's enough! That finishes it! Here's your twenty pence back! You can't have my horse!

CLEVER DICK Twenty pence! What are you talking about? You mean fifty pence. You said we could have the horse for fifty pence, and now you've only give us back twenty.

MEAN OLD MAN Uncle Bouki only gave me twenty pence. He said he'd give me the rest when he came to collect the horse.

CLEVER DICK Oh no! You told him it would cost fifty pence. So fifty pence is what you have to give back. And if you don't give it back, we'll take the horse.

UNCLE BOUKI Yes, we'll take the horse. But, oh dear! Where shall we put grandma when we all ride the horse to market? We must fit grandma on to the horse somewhere.

MEAN OLD MAN Take fifty pence, Clever Dick. Here you are. Take fifty pence and get away from my horse. I'm taking him home. Good-bye. ★

CLEVER DICK What a joke that was! I can't stop laughing. ★

UNCLE BOUKI That was good. Oh, we did play a trick on Mean Old Man.

CLEVER DICK I'm going home now, Uncle Bouki. But what a joke that was! I don't think I'll ever stop laughing. ★

UNCLE BOUKI What a joke that was! I gave him twenty pence and he gave me fifty pence back. I can't stop laughing! ★ I just want to feel all that lovely money in my pocket . . . Heh, but I haven't got any money in my pocket! . . . . Clever Dick's got it! The fifty pence is all in Clever Dick's pocket. He's got the fifty pence. CLEVER DICK'S GOT THE FIFTY PENCE IN HIS POCKET.

So who was the trick played on?

SNIP, SNAP, SNOVER
THIS BOOK'S OVER . . .

But you can find more stories like this in
Folk Tales for Reading and Telling *by Leila Berg, published by Brockhampton Press.*